PRECIPITATION

REVISED AND UPDATED

Measuring the Weather

Alan Rodgers and Angella Streluk

Heinemann
LIBRARY

Chicago, Illinois

Customer Service 888-454-2279
Visit our website at www.heinemannraintree.com

Designed by: Michelle Lisseter and Fiona MacColl
Originated by Modern Age
Printed and bound in China by South China Printing Company

11 10 09 08 07
10 9 8 7 6 5 4 3 2 1

New edition ISBNs: 978-1-4329-0073-1 (hardcover)
                       978-1-4329-0079-3 (paperback)

The Library of Congress has cataloged the first edition as follows:
Rodgers, Alan, 1958-
    Precipitation / Alan Rodgers and Angella Streluk
    p. cm. -- Measuring the weather)
Summary: An introduction to the different types of precipitation and explains how precipitation is related to weather. Includes bibliographical references and index.
    ISBN 1-58810-688-8 (hardcover) -- ISBN 1-40340-128-4 (paperback)
1. Precipitation (meteorology) -- Juvenile literature. [1. Precipitation (meteorology)] I. Streluk, Angella, 1961- II. Title.
QC920 .R64 2002
551.57'7--dc21

                     2002004018

Acknowledgements
The publishers would like to thank the following for permission to reproduce photographs: Alan Rodgers p. 17; Bruce Coleman Collection p. 4; Corbis pp. 7 (Corbis/Lester Lefkowitz), 9 (Reuters), 12 (Dean Conger); FLPA p. 18; Heather Angel p. 13; Pictor p. 29; Popperfoto pp. 27, 28; Robert Harding p. 25; Science Photo Library pp. 19, 20, 21, 26; Stefan Streluk p. 14; The National Met Office/W A Bentley p. 16; The National Met Office/M Grinnell p. 24; Trip/H Rogers p. 10.

Cover photographs reproduced with permission of Telegraph Colour Library and Tudor Photography.

Our thanks to Jacquie Syvret of the Met Office for her assistance during the preparation of this book.

Contents

You can find words in bold, **like this**, in the glossary.

Water Everywhere!

Did you know that the oceans hold roughly 94 percent of the world's water? These oceans play an important part in the weather. The weather is like a giant machine. The Sun and the oceans together drive this weather machine on Earth. The weather causes the water on Earth to change from liquid into **water vapor**, and in cold places it freezes into a solid. These changes form part of the **water cycle**. The movement of water as rain, snow, and hail is all part of the weather process.

Water is very important for all living things. Not enough rainfall is bad, but too much is just as much of a disaster. **Meteorologists** therefore spend a lot of time studying water in its different forms.

Looking at the Earth from space shows the large proportion of the planet that is covered by water.

Clouds move water from one place to another. They are made up of millions of gallons of water vapor and swirling air. Not all clouds produce rain and, even when they do, not all of it reaches the ground. Looking at the different types of clouds can be very interesting and informative.

Weather and climate

Weather and **climate** are not the same thing. The term weather means what happens from day to day (for example, sun and rain). It also includes those events that are unusual and unexpected (such as a violent storm). **Data** is collected for many years to determine the pattern of the weather in a specific area. This weather pattern through the seasons makes up that area's climate.

Meteorologists use symbols to represent different types of weather. These symbols are recognized all over the world so that meteorologists can exchange data. The symbols used by professional weather forecasters are often simplified for use on television and in newspapers.

Be careful!

Do not look directly at the Sun when studying the weather. Never take shelter under trees during a thunderstorm, because they could be hit by lightning.

*These are the internationally understood symbols used by meteorologists to represent **precipitation**.*

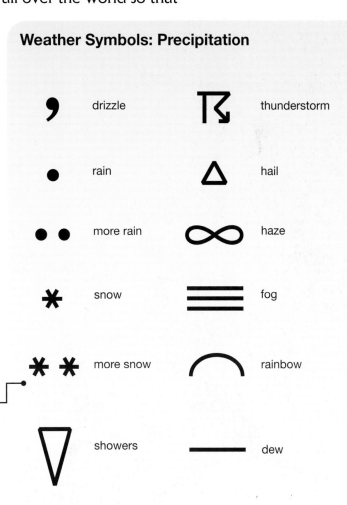

Weather Symbols: Precipitation

❜	drizzle	⚡	thunderstorm
●	rain	△	hail
● ●	more rain	∞	haze
✳	snow	≡	fog
✳ ✳	more snow	⌒	rainbow
▽	showers	—	dew

The Water Cycle

The water cycle is the system in which water moves and changes between its different forms. When we see water moving as it rains, we are only seeing a small part of the water cycle. Water also changes its form. Sometimes it will be water vapor in the **atmosphere**. Sometimes it **condenses** and becomes liquid again. Most of the world's water is in the oceans. Almost all of the rest is found in the polar regions, where it stays mostly as ice.

The water cycle works like this. The sun evaporates the moisture from the oceans, lakes, the land, and plants. Eighty-five percent of the moisture in the atmosphere comes from the seas and oceans. The rest evaporates from plants and moist lands, such as swamps. The evaporated water rises into the atmosphere. At cooler temperatures, the water vapor condenses into tiny **droplets** of water, creating clouds.

The Water Cycle

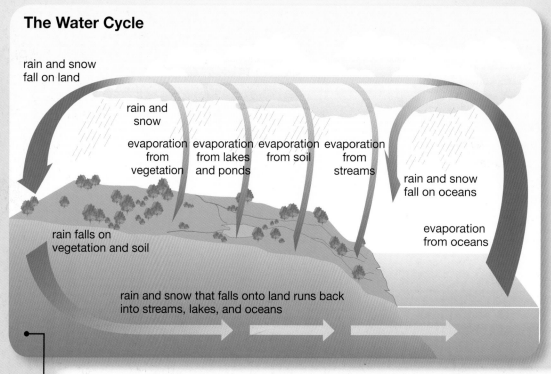

rain and snow fall on land

rain and snow

evaporation from vegetation   evaporation from lakes and ponds   evaporation from soil   evaporation from streams

rain and snow fall on oceans

rain falls on vegetation and soil

evaporation from oceans

rain and snow that falls onto land runs back into streams, lakes, and oceans

This diagram shows the water cycle. When rain or snow falls, some of the water evaporates almost immediately from wherever it lands. Other water runs into rivers, lakes, and oceans before eventually evaporating. The evaporated water enters the atmosphere, where it condenses to form clouds. Soon it will fall as rain or snow again.

Clouds release their water in certain conditions. When clouds are blown over higher land, or warm air forces them to rise, the water can fall as rain. If it is very cold, it will fall as hail or snow. Some rain falls in the ocean, and a large proportion of rain falls on land sloping up from the coast.

Much of the rain that falls onto land eventually makes its way to streams and then to large rivers. It eventually returns to the ocean and the entire water cycle begins again.

Hydroelectric dams

Heavy rain falling on hills and mountains can produce fast-flowing rivers. Many of these rivers have dams built across them with **hydroelectric** power stations inside them. These power stations use the water to produce electricity. The electricity produced in this way is environmentally friendly because it does not use up world resources, such as oil.

Dams provide environmentally friendly energy because they do not give off any greenhouse gases. However, they are not always good for people living near them. When dams are built they produce large lakes of water that will power the dam. These lakes may cover places where people live, so that they will have to move away and live in a new place.

Why Is It Raining Here?

The proper name for water that falls from clouds is precipitation. Water can fall in various forms, including **drizzle**, rain, **freezing rain**, and snow.

For it to rain, tiny molecules of water vapor need to form around very small particles of **matter**. These particles are usually tiny pieces of dust, pollutants, or ocean salt. If the atmosphere were completely pure, with no pollution or dirt, it would never rain! Combined with the water, the particles form droplets. These droplets do not fall right away—they are so tiny that air currents can keep them suspended in the air. The air within a cloud is always moving, carrying water droplets and ice crystals within it. During all this movement, many ice crystals and water droplets collide and join together. When they are too heavy to stay in the air, they fall to the ground. If it is warm, they will fall as rain. However, if there are violent **updrafts** and **downdrafts**, like in a big thunderstorm, the precipitation may eventually fall as frozen droplets, called hail.

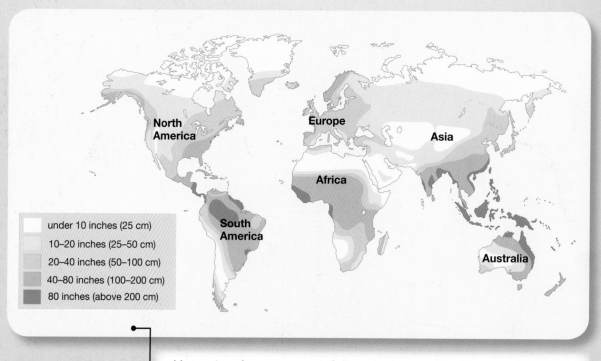

North America

Europe

Asia

Africa

South America

Australia

- under 10 inches (25 cm)
- 10–20 inches (25–50 cm)
- 20–40 inches (50–100 cm)
- 40–80 inches (100–200 cm)
- 80 inches (above 200 cm)

Measuring the average rainfall over a period of time shows that there is a pattern to where rain falls. This map shows yearly rainfall patterns.

Certain conditions are needed for precipitation to occur. There must be plenty of moisture in the atmosphere along with rising air. Together, this forms clouds. Precipitation occurs when clouds move to a height where it is cold. They can do this in two ways. Sometimes, clouds rise up the side of a large object, such as a mountain. In this case, the rain they produce is called **orographic** rain. Other times, warm air currents drive the clouds up to colder parts of the sky. This produces **convective** rain.

Lake effect

Sometimes in the winter, a cold dry wind blows across a large area of very warm water. On its journey, it collects large amounts of moisture. Fog forms above the water. The warmth from the water forces air up, and clouds appear. As these clouds approach the shore and hills, they are forced up even farther. This cools the clouds, and they deposit snow onto places near the areas of water. This phenomenon is known as lake-effect snow and it often happens in North America where heavy snow falls on cities near the Great Lakes.

Any large area of water will affect the local climate. In the case of lake-effect snow, the snowfall can be very spectacular.

Measuring Rainfall

One of the main instruments for measuring rainfall is a rain **gauge**. The measuring cup inside the gauge has a scale that shows how much rain has fallen. The **scale** must be in inches or millimeters. This shows the depth of rain that has fallen over the area.

Making a rain gauge

You can collect useful weather data with a simple homemade rain gauge. You can make one from an empty plastic soft drink bottle. Try to use one that has a diameter of 5 inches (127 millimeters), which is the correct size for a rain gauge. Carefully cut the top off. It will make an excellent funnel for collecting the rain. Turn it upside down with the narrow part sitting inside the rest of the bottle.

For more accurate results, you can buy an inexpensive rain gauge. You can then compare your homemade rain gauge's readings to those from the rain gauge you purchased.

Professional meteorologists use a rain gauge like this one. The outer container keeps the water from evaporating. An inner measuring container measures the rainfall accurately.

BE ACCURATE!

- Put your rain gauge where nothing blocks the rainfall.
- Place the rain gauge on a flat surface so that you can read it easily.
- Read the gauge with your eyes level with the scale.
- Measure the depth of the rain collected in inches or millimeters.

It is important to place your rain gauge where it will collect the most rainfall. Large objects, such as trees, can block the rain. You can try to find the best location by placing several rain gauges around an area. The results can then be compared. The rain gauge that collects the most rain is in the best place. As a general rule, calculate the height of the nearest tall object. The rain gauge should be located two-and-a-half times this height away from that object. For example, if a tree is 16 feet (5 meters) tall, the rain gauge needs to be 40 feet (12.5 meters) away from the tree.

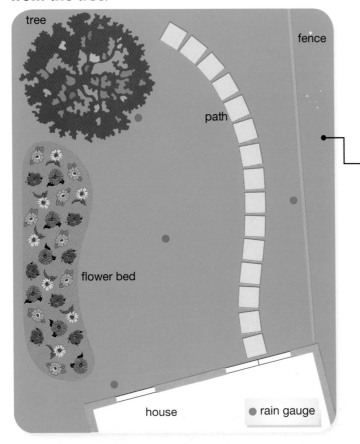

tree

fence

path

flower bed

house ● rain gauge

Make a drawing of your test sites for your rain gauges. Label each one and record the daily depth of rain there. Which gauge collects the most rain? This is the best place for a rain gauge.

Rain and Drizzle

How wet can you get? You may think that drizzle is not very wet, but if you spend any amount of time in it you will be soaked, just as if you were in a **downpour** of rain. Both rain and drizzle are forms of precipitation. The size and shape of the precipitation, the temperature inside the cloud, and how far rain travels inside the clouds before it falls from the sky all affect how rain falls.

Showers usually come from rounded, heaped (**cumulus**) clouds. Drizzle usually comes from low clouds. Rain that falls for a long period of time comes from layered (**stratus**) clouds. The main difference between rain and drizzle is the size of the droplets that fall on the ground. The average diameter of a raindrop is just under 0.1 inches (2 millimeters), whereas the much smaller individual drizzle droplet is 0.01 inches (0.2 millimeters). Rain often starts as snow while it is inside the cloud, but as it falls to a lower, warmer part of the sky, it melts and lands as rain.

This sudden downpour is very heavy, but it will only last a short time. If it were drizzling, it would last much longer.

Rainbows

A rainbow is one of nature's most wonderful shows. It appears when two things happen at the same time: the Sun shines at an appropriate angle, and droplets of rain fall. As the raindrops fall, they split up the sunlight into the colors of the rainbow (called the spectrum). A lot of raindrops falling at the same time give the impression of a continuous bow of color—the rainbow.

A rainbow can be made outside with a fine spray from a water hose or sprinkler. When the angles of the spray and the Sun are correctly lined up, an artificial rainbow can be seen.

TRY THIS YOURSELF!

```
You can try this if the rainfall is light.
• Lay out a sheet of light-colored paper in
  the rain.
• Observe the pattern the rain makes on the paper.
• To make the record permanent, take a pencil and
  draw around the drops before they dry.
• Is there a pattern?
```

Humidity

Humidity is the term used to describe the amount of water in the atmosphere. Meteorologists need to know the water content of the air so that they know whether clouds or fog are likely to form. There will not be rain unless there is a significant amount of water in the air. This varies in different places and in different conditions. The amount of water vapor in the air is measured as humidity on a scale from zero to one hundred and is given as a percentage. This percentage is known as relative humidity. The higher the percentage, the more water vapor is in the air.

In certain places, like banks, museums, and libraries, low humidity is a good thing, because it is important that paper and books are kept dry. In these places, the relative humidity may be monitored in case it gets too damp.

There are certain levels of humidity that are more comfortable for humans. We can put up with high temperatures as long as it is dry. But if it is hot and the air has a lot of moisture in it (high humidity), then it is uncomfortable for most people and animals.

In the deserts of Arizona, there is very little moisture in the air or ground, so the relative humidity is very low. Many airplanes are stored there by the United States Air Force because there is no need to cover them with waterproof wrappings.

TRY THIS YOURSELF!

Make a simple **hygrometer**—an instrument for measuring relative humidity.

- Use two accurate thermometers to read the same temperature in the same place.
- Mount them close to each other, allowing the air to flow freely around them.
- Tie a square of material to the bulb of one of the thermometers with a piece of fine string.
- Put the loose ends of the string into a small container of distilled water.
- You now have a wet bulb thermometer and a dry bulb thermometer.
- Make a note of the readings on both thermometers.
- Look up the humidity on a Relative Humidity Chart like the one below.
- Let's say the dry bulb temperature is 62°F and the wet bulb temperature is 57°F. Use your finger to trace down the column under 62°F and another finger to trace across the row from 57°F. The relative humidity is where these two lines meet. In this case the relative humidity is 74 percent.

Relative Humidity Chart						
Dry bulb temperature / Wet bulb temperature	61°F	62°F	63°F	64°F	65°F	66°F
55°F	68%	64%	60%	56%	52%	48%
56°F	73%	69%	64%	60%	56%	53%
57°F	78%	74%	69%	65%	61%	57%
58°F	84%	79%	74%	70%	66%	61%

Snow and Sleet

Snow is a form of precipitation. There are many kinds of snow—from fine and dry to wet and large flakes. The size and shape of the precipitation, the temperature inside the cloud, and how far snow travels inside the clouds before it falls all affect the type of snow that we see.

Snow forms when there are ice crystals in thick clouds. As they fall through the clouds, these tiny crystals combine to become bigger flakes. If it is cold on the way down, the precipitation stays in the form of snow. If it is not quite cold enough, there will be a mixture of snow and rain by the time it reaches the ground.

*Snow crystals seen under great magnification have beautiful six-sided patterns. These can include stars, **prisms**, and columns.*

Different types of snow

Winter sports enthusiasts appreciate the subtle differences in types of snow. Some types of snow provide better surfaces for skiing than others. Dry powdery snow falls when it is so cold that ice crystals do not thaw, freeze, and combine. This is ideal for skiing. However, when fine dry powdery snow falls on top of old snow that is icy and frozen, it does not stick. This means it can slip in large movements of snow called **avalanches**. These can suddenly sweep down mountain slopes and bury people.

MEASURING SNOW

- Depth of snow is measured with a ruler.
- Use a metal ruler.
- Measure snow that is still smooth.
- Avoid snow that has drifted or been **scored** by the wind and blown into ridges.
- Hold the ruler vertically in the snow.
- Note the reading in inches or centimeters.
- Take two more readings and take an average (add the three readings and divide the number by three).
- Clear a fresh area for future readings. If there is more snow, you want to be able to measure it from ground level.

It is important to read the ruler when it is vertical. If possible, take the reading near where you have placed your rain gauge. This means that you will be in a clear, open space.

Hail

Hailstones are not made of stone, but frozen, layered clumps of ice! Most of them are about the size of a pea, between 0.2 and 0.4 inches (5 and 10 millimeters) across. The largest hailstone ever recorded in the United States (measured by circumference rather than weight) fell from a storm in Aurora, Nebraska, on June 22, 2003. It measured 7 inches (17.8 centimeters) wide and 18.7 inches (47.6 centimeters) in circumference. In 1986, a hailstorm in Bangladesh, India, produced hail weighing more than 2 pounds (1 kilogram).

All around the world, hail can cause damage to property and animals, as well as people. In the 1950s, a woman in Canada wrote to her niece in England:

"Can you imagine a field of wheat two feet [61 centimeters] high at twenty past six, and at half past six the field looked like a ploughed field."

The entire crop was destroyed. So although hailstorms rarely last more than a few minutes, they can cause an enormous amount of damage.

Even when hailstones are not very big, they can cause terrible damage. This is because they come down with force from a great height. The crop damage seen here was caused in a few minutes.

Hail clouds

Clouds that produce hail mainly form in the strong **up-currents** of spring and summer. In places with very warm temperatures, the hailstones melt before they reach the ground. Hail is formed within giant thunderclouds. Because the air currents are so violent and temperatures vary in different parts of the cloud, the water droplets inside the cloud become very cold. As the hail grows in size, it falls, but before it reaches the bottom of the cloud, gusts of wind take it up again. There it gets another coating of ice. As it goes up and down inside the cloud, the hailstone melts and freezes. This continues until it is so heavy that it falls to the ground.

TRY THIS YOURSELF!

- Get a hailstone. Keep it cool or it will melt.
- Get an adult to cut it in half.
- Look closely at it using a microscope or a magnifying glass.
- Look at the alternate layers of clear and frosted ice.

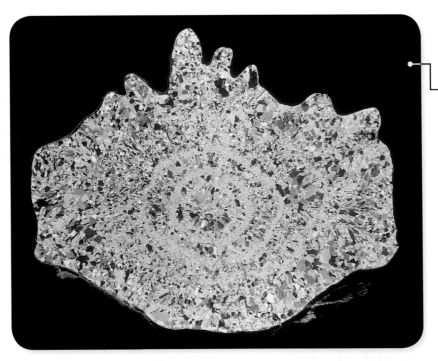

The more powerful the microscope, the more you will be able to see the alternate layers inside a hailstone. The movement of the hailstone rising and falling inside the cloud causes these layers.

Rain Clouds

Various types of clouds carry rain. The shape, size, and height of these different clouds can give clues to the kind of weather they may bring. These characteristics also helps us name clouds.

Layered clouds let their precipitation fall gently, as drizzle. This drizzle usually continues for very long periods of time. Medium-height, layered clouds (altostratus) produce rain only when they are very thick. Low and dark layered clouds (nimbostratus) bring downpours of heavier rain that can last a long time.

Dark gray, puffy clouds release their precipitation very energetically, often as a short downpour. They can blow over quite quickly, taking the rain with them. The cumulus cloud is the main rain cloud of this type. Large round, black clouds are called cumulonimbus clouds. These can bring storms with heavy rain or snow. There is often a noticeable drop in temperature just before it rains.

These towering cumulonimbus clouds stretch up through the sky. They can bring thunder and lightning.

Satellites

Meteorologists use **satellites** to show them exactly where cloud formations are. It is very helpful to know well in advance where the clouds are, especially when they are out at sea, where there are fewer **weather stations** to collect weather data. The satellite images give a lot of information about the type and behavior of the clouds. By using special cameras, the satellites can see more than an ordinary camera. For example, satellites can see the difference in heat in different parts of the clouds. This may tell meteorologists what is happening in the clouds.

Some groups set up their own satellite systems. This can be expensive, but the images are spectacular and give a lot of information about the future of weather patterns. Many universities and weather agencies regularly display their satellite images on the Internet, with explanations of what they mean.

This color-coded satellite image shows the location of a severe storm. The colors show whether or not the cloud is likely to be dropping precipitation. These images can be used to follow the movement of weather systems in order to make a weather report.

Take a look at the website below to see satellite images of the weather:

http://www.weather.gov

Frontal Systems

Frontal systems are shown on weather maps so that people know what weather to expect. When you look at a weather map, you will see special lines called isobars. These lines connect areas with the same **air pressure**. Special lines with curved symbols on them show a warm **front**. Lines with triangular symbols along them show a cold front. A front is the edge of a large body of air. These fronts bring special weather.

Warm fronts

A warm front approaches with its front edge high in the sky. The trailing part of the front slopes downward. The first signs of the approaching warm front are the feathery **cirrus** clouds high in the sky that then spread out into **cirrostratus** clouds. Altostratus and nimbostratus follow at the point where the warm front slopes to the ground. These clouds bring rain with them.

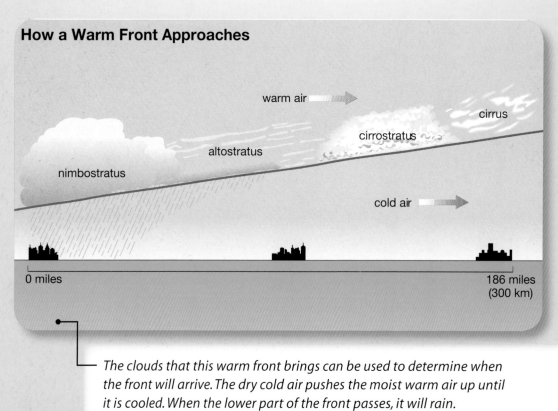

How a Warm Front Approaches

warm air

cirrus

cirrostratus

altostratus

nimbostratus

cold air

0 miles

186 miles
(300 km)

The clouds that this warm front brings can be used to determine when the front will arrive. The dry cold air pushes the moist warm air up until it is cooled. When the lower part of the front passes, it will rain.

Cold fronts

A cold front approaches with much less warning than a warm front. It curves up from the surface of the ground, as you can see in the illustration. At first, there are cirrus, cirrostratus, and **altocumulus** clouds. These are followed quickly by the cumulonimbus cloud, which brings downpours, and sometimes hail and thunderstorms.

You can use your knowledge of fronts to help forecast the weather. By watching for the sequences of cloud types, you will be able to tell when a warm or cold front is approaching. You may see on the weather forecasts on television that a front is approaching. You can then look at the clouds and see how long it will be until the rain arrives. If you see cirrus clouds in a blue sky, you will know that this could be the start of a front bringing rain.

How a Cold Front Approaches

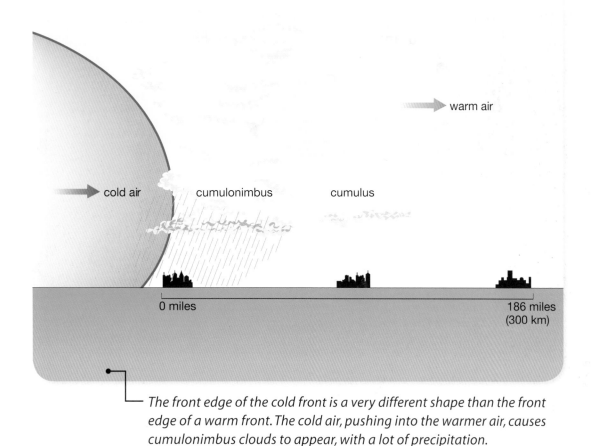

The front edge of the cold front is a very different shape than the front edge of a warm front. The cold air, pushing into the warmer air, causes cumulonimbus clouds to appear, with a lot of precipitation.

Microbursts

Microbursts are dramatic weather events that cause strong bursts of wind. Microbursts often occur as a result of isolated rain showers or thunderstorms. There are two types of microbursts: wet and dry. Wet microbursts occur in wet conditions and dry microbursts occur in dry conditions.

In a dry microburst, a column of rain suddenly falls from a cloud into the dry air beneath. The rain quickly evaporates. This evaporation cools the air. The cool air is heavy and sinks, making a powerful downward wind under the cloud. The wind hits the ground and spreads out, traveling about another 2.5 miles (4 kilometers). This wind might last only from 5 to 20 minutes, but it can reach speeds of up to 135 mph (215 kph). However, a distant observer may only notice a dry microburst disturbing the dust on the ground.

Wet microbursts occur when it is raining very heavily. In these microbursts, a lot of the rain reaches the ground along with a downdraft. The wind and rain hits the ground with such force that it produces another wind that goes out sideways. This sideways wind is called windshear.

In this wet microburst, you can see the downpour of rain that causes the strong burst of downward wind.

A dangerous kind of weather

Microbursts can be dangerous for airplanes, especially when they are landing or taking off. The powerful winds they produce can cause airplanes to have serious problems.

Work is being done to predict microbursts. If the temperature at ground level is very different from the temperature in the air, this means that microbursts are more likely. Indexes are being developed. These are systems that will help to predict when the weather conditions needed for the two types of microbursts are present. These indexes include the Dry Microburst Index (DMI) and the Microburst Day Potential Index (MDPI).

Understanding the local weather at airports is very important. As airplanes prepare for takeoff or landing, information about the weather is passed on to the pilots, and they can then make decisions about the effects of the weather on the safety of the plane.

Rain and Snow Warnings

Rain and snow have a big effect on people's lives, so it is important to know when they will occur. Professional meteorologists try to gather a lot of information about the weather from as wide an area as possible. They can warn people about the possibility of bad weather. This is very important when there is going to be a lot of precipitation. When monitoring the weather, meteorologists share the data they collect and pass on warnings to each other.

Some weather watchers use devices called **radar**. The radar bounces special waves off the clouds into a receiver. These show where a storm is and which way it is traveling. Satellites in space can also spot a storm developing out at sea. As a storm comes closer inland, radar stations can continue to follow it. It is important to try to predict serious weather conditions. In June of 2006, a devastating series of storms struck the northeastern part of the United States. Roads and bridges were wiped out, buildings were destroyed, and several deaths were reported. Some areas received as much as 12 inches (30 centimeters) of rain in a six-day span. The ability to predict such severe storms could save property and lives.

Regional, national, and international weather forecasts begin with readings taken at weather stations in many different locations. This weather station has its own radar equipment, which is housed inside a special dome.

Hurricanes, floods, and snow

Hurricanes are tropical storms. They can bring large amounts of rain that can cause terrible damage. Meteorologists receive hourly satellite pictures. If thunderstorms look as though they are developing into a hurricane, satellite images are used to look for signs of rotation. Hurricanes are monitored and warnings are passed to ships, aircraft, and the general public.

Flood warnings can be very helpful. One way of predicting flooding is to study rainfall at the starting points of rivers. Measuring stations can be placed along rivers. They measure the amount of water flowing by, and measure the water in all parts of the river. This data helps to predict flooding farther down the river.

Snow also needs to be monitored. If a lot of snow falls in the winter, it could cause flooding when it melts. Snowfall is also monitored to see if it is stable. This means it is not likely to cause avalanches. These can destroy entire villages.

If people are warned early enough about bad weather, they can make preparations to reduce damage to life and property. Here, residents of North Carolina prepare for a hurricane.

Floods and Drought

The term drought means that no rain has fallen where it would normally be expected to fall. The amount of rain expected depends on the climate of the area. A dry summer for one country would be considered a wet one for another country. Drought definitions in the United States vary from region to region. In Europe and other countries where rain normally falls all year round, if it does not rain, or rains less than 0.01 inches (0.2 millimeters) per day, for 15 days in a row, a drought is declared.

Very often in the summer months, an area of high pressure will stay over a region and will not move. While this high air pressure stays still, the normal **depressions** that bring rain are forced into different areas.

Bringing relief

For many people in Africa, long periods of drought bring suffering. Crops cannot grow, and water supplies dry up. In places that suffer long droughts, attempts can be made to encourage the formation of rain clouds.

Research is continuing into the best ways to bring rain to areas that need it. These airplanes are trying to cause precipitation— one of them is spraying chemicals to help create rain.

One of the ways in which clouds naturally form is by water droplets sticking to tiny particles in the atmosphere. If there are not enough of these particles, airplanes can spray particles of harmless chemicals into the clouds. The droplets then form around these, and rain may follow. However, this process relies on the fact that there is already water vapor in the air, so it is not very reliable.

Many countries in the world alternate between being hot and dry and warm and wet. These countries rely on receiving a lot of their annual rainfall in a short period of time. The people of the Indian subcontinent call this great rainfall period the monsoons. The monsoons are a seasonal wind system, bringing wind and rain. This arrives in May and continues for six months. Its arrival breaks a long hot dry spell, bringing relief to millions of people.

Whatever type of precipitation people experience—rain, hail, sleet, or snow—it seems to be a topic that interests everybody. When water falls from the sky in any form it affects people, plants, and animals. The more you know about it, the more amazing it seems.

This heavy rain is called a monsoon. People are usually pleased when it comes, because it ends a long spell of dry weather.

Glossary

air pressure pressure, at the surface of the Earth, caused by the weight of the air in the atmosphere

altocumulus type of cloud, found in patches in the middle height of the sky, usually white or gray. This type of cloud is shaped in puffy heaps.

atmosphere gases that surround our planet. They are kept in place by gravity.

avalanche snow, with ice and rock, that travels quickly down a mountain side

cirrostratus type of cloud found very high in the sky. It is thin and transparent and made of ice crystals.

cirrus highest form of clouds, made up of ice crystals in thin feather-like shapes

climate weather conditions in an area over a long period of years

condense when water vapor returns to its liquid state

convective vertical movement, especially upwards, of warm air

cumulus type of cloud, consisting of rounded heaps with a darker horizontal base

data facts that can be investigated to get information

depression area with low air pressure readings (a cyclone, for example)

downdraft current of air moving in a downward direction

downpour heavy fall of rain

drizzle small, light rain

droplets little drops

freezing rain rain that freezes when it hits the ground or other objects

front front edge of an air mass, where it meets air of a different temperature

frontal system area where air masses of different temperatures and humidity meet

gauge measuring equipment, in this case for measuring rain

hydroelectric electricity produced by means of water power

hygrometer instrument for measuring the relative humidity of the air

matter material that things are made of

meteorologist somebody who studies the weather by gathering and analyzing data

orographic related to mountains

precipitation moisture or water vapor that condenses and falls as rain, hail, or snow

prism object or material that splits light into separate colors

radar use of radio signals to find out about objects, including how far away they are

satellite man-made device that orbits the Earth, receiving and transmitting information

scale numbers used to represent measurement on instruments such as thermometers

scored marked with a notch or incised groove, in this case one made in the snow by the wind, which makes the snow uneven

stratus forming a layer

up-current rising current of air

updraft current of air moving in an upward direction

water cycle cycle in which water from the sea evaporates into the atmosphere, condenses, and falls to Earth as rain or snow. It then evaporates directly back into the atmosphere or returns to the sea by rivers.

water vapor water in the form of gas

weather station collection of weather instruments that measures the weather regularly

Find Out More

Make a rainbow on a sunny day. In your kitchen, work with an adult to fill a bowl of water and place a mirror at 45 degrees. Put the bowl, with the water and mirror, in strong sunlight. Adjust its position until a wonderful rainbow appears on the ceiling or wall.

Events in the northeast United States in June 2006 produced dramatic flash flooding. This started a debate about whether or not the heavy rain was a result of climate change. Find out about the effects of the floods and see if you agree that climate change might be partly to blame.

Sometimes the water in the air can absorb pollution in the air. This can have serious consequences, making the rain into a type of weak acid. You can use a special acid rain kit or a pH kit to test the pH of the rain in your area. Readings below pH5 are considered acidic. Find out what acid rain does to living things and to architecture.

More books to read

Frisch, Joy. *Temperature: Understanding Science*. Mankato, MN: Smart Apple Media, 2002.

Rupp, Rebecca. *Weather*. North Adams, MA: Storey Publishing, 2003.

Spilsbury, Louise and Richard Spilsbury. *Raging Floods*. Chicago: Heinemann Library, 2003.

Taylor, Barbara. *Weather and Climate*. New York: Kingfisher, 2002.

Websites

http://www.nws.noaa.gov
The national weather service website has tons of information on the weather. There is a students page that contains links to many other weather websites.

http://www.weather.com
This website has a lot of information on the weather. You can enter your zip code to view a weather forecast for your area.

Index